The Sporting Life of Track Hodges

The Sporting Life of Track Hodges

By Donny Hodges
Illustrated by Kendall Tabor Jr

MILL CITY PRESS

Dedicated to and Inspired by Trey and Jack Hodges

Mill City Press
2301 Lucien Way #415
Maitland, FL 32751
407.339.4217
www.millcitypress.net

© 2019 by Donny Hodges
Illustrated by Kendall Tabor Jr.

All rights reserved solely by the author. The author guarantees all contents are original and do not infringe upon the legal rights of any other person or work. No part of this book may be reproduced in any form without the permission of the author. The views expressed in this book are not necessarily those of the publisher.

Printed in the United States of America.

LCCN: 2019-916821

ISBN-13: 978-1-5456-3154-6

This is Track...

Track loves to play sports. Football is his favorite. He loves to run the ball, throw and catch the ball, and even kick the ball. He loves football so much that he sleeps with one every night.

So you can imagine how he felt when it was the last play of the football game, and his *big* chance to win, and this happened . . .

Coach called the team to huddle up. Track hoped he would get to run the ball, but the coach told him to block for the runner. Track could imagine so many more exciting positions to play instead of just being a "blocker".

But the team broke the huddle before Track could say anything so he just clapped his hands and said, "Let's get this done."

They snapped the ball and the runner followed Track toward the end zone.

The runner was tackled at the one yard line as the clock ran out. So close!

Track's team lost the game. Coach thanked everyone for playing their best.

His words were nice and all, but Track was still disappointed. *Losing stinks more than the time I was sick on field trip day*, he thought.

"Thanks for the ride, Track's Dad," said Track's friend, Tommy.

"You don't have to thank me, Tommy," said Dad. "We love having you ride with us to all of the games. You guys want to stop for ice cream?"

"Who can eat after a loss?" Track asked. He could imagine so many other more important things he should be doing instead of eating ice cream.

"Thanks, Track's Dad. I had a couple of hot dogs today, but I always have room for ice cream," said Tommy.

"The game just finished. When did you have time for a couple of hot dogs?" Track asked.

"Hmm…Sometime between the 3rd and 4th quarter, I think."

"I'd like a hot fudge sundae with whipped cream, extra peanuts, extra cherries, sprinkles, marshmallows, and french fries on top, please," said Tommy.

"Ummm, we don't have french fries here," said the girl at the counter. "This is an ice cream shop."

"Oh, that's okay. I brought some of my own from the game."

"Track, what did you think when the coach decided to let another player run the ball on the last play," asked Dad. "I know you love to run the ball."

"**Coach told me to block.** I just wanted to win, so I tried to do what he said, but I didn't do a good enough job."

"Do you want me to talk to your coach?" asked Dad.

"I don't think so. I will just work harder at practice."

After dropping off Tommy, Dad said, "I have great news!"

This made Track perk up.

"Our favorite football team is playing tonight. We can watch the game, eat pizza, and have a fun family night."

When they got home, Dad looked around the house with disappointment.

Track hadn't done any of his chores.

Track explained that he would do his chores later and made several excuses.

Dad listened to Track, but didn't change his mind. When Track was done talking, Dad clapped his hands and said, "Let's get this done!"

Track was not amused, but Dad thought it was very funny.

Track could imagine so many other things he would rather be doing instead of his chores.

"Can I watch the game now?"

"I'm all done with my chores," said Track.

Dad shook his head. The game was over. It had been an exciting game and Track would have loved it.

"Sorry, Track. If you had done your job when you were supposed to, we could have all watched the game and had fun. It's bedtime now," said Dad.

The next day back at football practice,

Track and Tommy were doing their drills, but when Tommy got the ball he kept running toward the wrong end zone!

The coach said, "Tommy, why do you keep running the wrong way?"

"All those other guys are in my way if I run that way! It's so much easier to run when no one is in my way!" Tommy answered.

Coach slapped his forehead. "That's what your blocker is for. He makes the hole so that no one is in your way. Then you just run for it."

"Coach is right, Tommy," said Track.

Coach looked at Track and said, "Track, blocking is an important part of the game and you're a great blocker! We need you to be a full-time blocker and help our team win!"

Track thought for a minute and then replied, "Sure Coach! Just one thing. Do you think Tommy could play more during our games?"

Coach took off his hat
and scratched his head, thinking hard about it. After what seemed like forever, he said, "Sure, Track! As long as we can get him to run the right way!"

They both chuckled, but Track said, "Leave it to me, Coach!"

On the day of the big game, the coach called the team together to give them the plan.

Track would block.

"Tommy, we need you to run!" said Coach.

Tommy immediately started running around the field.

"No, Tommy," said Track. "You are going to run in the game, not now!"

"I don't know what to do," said Tommy.

"Just remember what coach said about finding the hole," said Track. "I'm your blocker today, and I'm going to make a big hole for you. That is my job! Just run right behind me, and you are going to be OK."

Track blocked as hard as he could.
He was great at blocking. The other team didn't know how to stop him.

The score was tied, and there was only time for one more play. Track knew that if he made a big enough hole, Tommy would follow.

And did Tommy ever follow Track! Tommy and Track rumbled and tumbled their way through the other team's defense. It was a sight to see and the crowd went crazy as Tommy happily crossed the goal line to score the game winning touchdown!

Track and Tommy had done their jobs well and they had never had so much fun!

After celebrating the big win, Track and his dad returned home. Dad looked around the house. Track had done all of his chores. Dad was surprised and very proud of Track.

With a big smile on his face, Dad gave Track a high-five.

"Great job with your chores, son," he said. "You did your job on the field and at home."

This made Track feel very proud.

"What made you do your chores without Mom or me asking you?" asked Dad.

"All week at practice, Coach had me block. I didn't really want to at first, but I trusted him. It turned out that when I did my best at my job it helped everyone else on the team to get better at their jobs too!" said Track.

"Our family is a team too, and when we all do our part, everything is better. Last week I let you and Mom down. You can count on me from now on. That is what teamwork is all about."

Because Track had done his chores, his family had time for a fun night. They watched an exciting football game, ate delicious pizza, and had a lively family game night!

This has been a really great day!

Maybe the best day of my life so far!

Better than I could ever imagine!

Track says, Think about it.

What is your job on your team?

How about at home?

Or at school?

Or even with your friends?

Your job, no matter how big or small, is very important.

And when you do your job well, it helps every team you play on . . . so "Let's Get It Done!"

See you at the game!

CPSIA information can be obtained
at www.ICGtesting.com
Printed in the USA
LVHW071611141119
637081LV00035B/1323/P